PowerKids Readers:
Nature Books™

Leaves

Kristin Ward

The Rosen Publishing Group's
PowerKids Press™
New York

For Thomas and Mak, with love

Published in 2000 by The Rosen Publishing Group, Inc.
29 East 21st Street, New York, NY 10010

First Edition

Book design: Michael de Guzman

Photo Credits: pp.1, 7, 9 © 1998 PhotoDisc; p. 5 © Digital Vision; p. 11 © Richard Laird/FPG International; pp. 13, 17 © Stephen Simpson/FPG International; p. 15 © Dennie Cody/FPG International; p. 19 © Roger Markham Smith/International Stock; p. 21 © Stan Ries/International Stock.

Ward, Kristin.
    Leaves / by Kristin Ward.
        p. cm. — (Nature books)
    Summary: Simple text and pictures describe the different shapes, sizes, and colors of leaves, as well as what happens to them in the spring and fall.
        ISBN 0-8239-5533-8
    1. Leaves Juvenile literature. [1. Leaves.] I. Title. II. Series: Nature books (New York, N.Y.)
QK649.W27   1999
581'.4'8—dc21   99-14630
                                                          CIP

Manufactured in the United States of America

Contents

Leaves grow on trees.

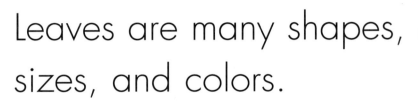

Leaves are many shapes,
sizes, and colors.

7

Some leaves are small and flat.
Other leaves are big and pointy.

9

Some leaves turn colors
in the fall.
Leaves can turn red,
yellow, and orange.

Some leaves stay green
in the fall.
Evergreen trees have
leaves that always stay
green.

In the fall, the wind blows leaves to the ground.

We rake the leaves into piles.

We scoop the leaves into bags.

In the spring, new leaves will grow on the trees.

Words to Know

BAG

LEAVES

PILE

RAKE

TREE

Here are more books to read about leaves:

Autumn Leaves
by Ken Robbins
Scholastic Trade

The Little Leaf
by Chana Sharfstein, illustrations by Rochelle
Blumenfeld
Hachai Publications

To learn more about leaves, check out this
Web site:
http://www.waterw.com/~science/october.
html

Index

Word Count: 84

Note to Librarians, Teachers, and Parents

PowerKids Readers (Nature Books) are specially designed to help emergent and beginning readers build their skills in reading for information. Simple vocabulary and concepts are paired with photographs of real kids in real-life situations or stunning, detailed images from the natural world around them. Readers will respond to written language by linking meaning with their own everyday experiences and observations. Sentences are short and simple, employing a basic vocabulary of sight words, as well as new words that describe objects or processes that take place in the natural world. Large type, clean design, and photographs corresponding directly to the text all help children to decipher meaning. Features such as a contents page, picture glossary, and index help children get the most out of PowerKids Readers. They also introduce children to the basic elements of a book, which they will encounter in their future reading experiences. Lists of related books and Web sites encourage kids to explore other sources and to continue the process of learning.